In the Panhandle

Poems 1975–2020

In the Panhandle

Poems 1975–2020

by

Reagan Upshaw

© 2023 Reagan Upshaw. All rights reserved.
This material may not be reproduced in any form, published,
reprinted, recorded, performed, broadcast,
rewritten or redistributed without
the explicit permission of Reagan Upshaw.
All such actions are strictly prohibited by law.

Cover design by Shay Culligan
Cover image "Buffalo Lake Texas Windmill"
at Wikimedia Commons

ISBN: 978-1-63980-373-6

Kelsay Books
502 South 1040 East, A-119
American Fork, Utah 84003
Kelsaybooks.com

For Roberta

Acknowledgements

The following poems first appeared, sometimes in different versions, in the magazines listed. My thanks to their editors.

Able Muse: "Jim Brodey"
The Agonist: "A Bestiary," "Dry," "Crosses"
American Journal of Poetry: "Saint Johnsbury"
Amethyst: "Aubade"
Atlanta Review: "Hay Fever"
Barefoot Muse: "The Queen"
Black River Poetry Review: "Matador"
Catskill Mountain Region Guide: "Greene County," "Too Hot Not to Cool Down"
Chronogram: "In the Panhandle"
E-Verse Radio: "The Toadstone"
Giants Play Well In The Drizzle: "Instructions"
Hamilton Stone Review: "Kitchen, Night," "Letters from Connie," "Alzheimer's," "Carnivore," "Mottes"
Hanging Loose: "Dashboard Pantheon"
Ithaca Lit: "Ohrwurm"
New Paltz Nation: "The Ogre"
Quadrant: "Voyager," "Brute Parasite," "Shotgun Wedding"
Rotary Dial: "The Water Lily"
Verse Virtual: "Inheritance," "Injun Country"

Contents

In the Panhandle   13

I

Matador   17
Brute Parasite   18
Brooklyn, July   19
Dashboard Pantheon   21

II

On the Cape   23

III Upon a Time

The Ogre   43
The Saint   44
The Soldier   45
The Devil's Grandmother   46
The Knight   47
The Woodsman   49
The Queen   50
The Fool   51
The Lord   52

IV

Hay Fever   55
Instructions   56
The Water Lily   57
Judgment   58
Greene County   59

V Mother and Son

Kitchen, Night	65
Letters from Connie	67
Alzheimer's	69
Inheritance	72

VI

Jim Brodey	75
Ohrwurm	78
Valhalla	79
Saint Johnsbury	80
The Toadstone	83
Too Hot Not to Cool Down	85
Dry	86
The Old Believers	88
Mottes	91
A Bestiary	92
Crosses	95
Endless Love	97
Injun Country	99
Carnivore	100
Aubade	102
Crib Song	104
Voyager	105
Shotgun Wedding	109
To a Dying Artist	110
Lights Out	113

In the Panhandle

It seemed that every native thing grew thorns
on my uncle's ranch—mesquite, cacti, goathead stickers.
Out back, beyond the barbed wire
that circled the house, a tiny stream
trickled from puddle to puddle,
belabored by sun and incessant wind,
escaping finally into the Palo Duro Canyon.
Its bed was barely three feet wide,
easily vaulted by children seeking arrowheads.
The cattle ignored its scant offering
as they plodded toward the windmill
with its tank of tepid water.
One year, my uncle told me,
When even the stingy rainfall did not come,
the stream failed completely, and
—who would have thought it?—
he found fish on its sand, little fish,
dead and dried up. Whoever dreamed
something could have lived in there?

Or in here?

I

Matador

When I'm with an angry woman,
I'm home. Amusement sours, interest fades,
and adoration I've never known what to do with,
but the anger of women has been
a passion I could count on, that moment
when the eyes widen, the smile
is sucked in. Then, the belt came down;
now, fingernails claw for my face,
pots and glasses whiz through the air.
I dodge or cajole, and in that moment
I know where I am.

Stand erect, and face the love
that paws and snorts, scenting blood.
Your mind is clear now, your senses
focused to a ring, while your offenses
glitter like a suit of lights,

Aye, toro. Toro.

Brute Parasite

The cuckoo's egg, laid in a foreign nest,
hatches into the goggle-eyed monster

who puts his back to the rightful eggs
and any naked, luckless chicks

and one by one, by dull instinct,
muscles them over the edge.

Consuming all the food his foster parents bring,
he soon swells to fill the nest,

incessantly bawling his two-note song:
Feed me. Feed me. Feed me.

And you, fat boy—who left you here?
You, instinctive parent—feed your foster child.

Brooklyn, July

The long day's force appeared to ease
at nightfall, and you went to bed
by an open window, hoping for
a deep, unbroken sleep. Instead,

three hours later you awake,
cocooned in heat. You roll to check
the time, put up your hand, and feel
sweat's beaded choker round your neck.

Were you to put the light on now
and turn, you'd see your silhouette
still sleeping on the pillowcase,
an image painted with your sweat.

You don't put on the light. You kick
the sheet off, turn the pillow, hear
the gates come down across the street
as the bartender locks the bar.

No hint of moving air. The only
objects moving are the drops
of sweat meandering through your scalp,
seeking to pool as one. Perhaps

the time has come for mastery.
Get up and shut the window, push
the buttons in the dark and feel
the regulated air's onrush?

Resist the urge. Lie still and watch
each number on the clock supplant
the last until, aestheticized,
your brain ignores the heat's affront.

Three hours from now, the light of dawn
will wake you, as a playful breeze
kisses your cheek and then your naked
nipples, belly, thighs, knees.

A sense of peace will float up with
the first cicada's sawing, far
above the traffic's susurration.
We can love the thing we are.

Dashboard Pantheon

To the left of the taxi meter,
secure to their magnets as Hope to her anchor,
four figures:

Mary—Not the Protestant Mary, nine months and one night of glory, followed by an ordinary life bearing the carpenter's children, ending a bent, old woman, but the Catholic Virgin, ever young, now tiny and magical as Tinker Bell.

St. Christopher—Proof that human need does not need proof. Disavowed by the church, he floats free of history, a nothing that protects something. Make no enemies, he seems to say. Better safe than sorry.

St. Roch—Different time, different plague, but he knows the ropes. Does his statue stand in shooting galleries and gay bars also? Or is it only when the mirror reflects his sores that the praying begins?

Big Bird—Overgrown, wide-eyed American innocence. Always seeking answers and eager to believe. And not yet demanding sacrifice, not yet out for blood.

Written in the time of AIDS

II

On the Cape

Artwork by Buzz Spector

1

Well, Buzz, here we are on the Cape.
The Cape, not the Cape of Horn, the
Cape of Good Hope, or even
the Cape of Zorro—sorry,
is that the way it's going to be with you here?
You, master of wordplay and,
with Peter Frank. the most audacious punster
I've ever met it my life. But your words
won't avail you here; *I* get to chat,
and *you* have to be the illustrator. Forgive me,
I know that's a dirty word to an artist,
like describing a poet as a rhymester
or a novelist as "a sensitive observer of life."
Enough. Shall we invoke the muse?
A poem of this length seems to demand it.
Oh, sexy one, let me write as I speak,
let me not lose my nerve and get poetic,
inspire me with the example of Schuyler,
Schjeldahl, and Koch, let me know
that this, too, can be poetry.

Five years it has taken me, five years
of torn-up sonnets & discarded triolets,
of nights awake talking & of reading
blear-eyed & lonely under a thousand
different lamps. Five years
of sitting & listening & waiting

& all for this: to write exactly as I speak.
I am ready now—what
is there to say?

I wrote that poem about 15 years ago,
but I haven't learned from it. Does one ever?
I still believe in sweat, still distrust
anything that comes easy. The Puritan heritage,
like believing that medicine for a cut
does no good unless it stings.
We're here on Cape Cod,
at Orleans, to be exact. It's August,
1987, and we've agreed to do a book.
The form will be epistolary, loose enough
for me to put in whatever I want;
a form, like Cape Cod, big enough to ramble in,
yet bounded by constraints that can be
delightful in themselves. The beaches, the bays,
like a postcard, and those
waves that are such a pleasure to dive under.
I love the surge of energy that enters your head
and runs out at your toes when you do that,
popping your body like a whip.
There are a lot of literary footprints in the sand.
Thoreau was here, though it's generally admitted
that *Cape Cod* is not one of his finest works.
Randall Jarrell spent some time here,
did you know that? What's the essential
Cape Cod poem? I can't think of one.
The closest thing to capture the feeling
is William Carlos Williams' poem "Nantucket."
I love that, don't you? To sum up a place
in ten lines packed with images.
I couldn't do that, though, that vision—
is it Imagist or Objectivist?—that forms and edits,
carefully removing the traces of the artist's hand,
leaving a perfect artifact. No,
my viewpoint of nature's that Egotistical

Sublime, as Keats said of Wordsworth.
The sea may grind these pebbles smooth
—pebbles, hell, they're rocks as big as my fist—
but it can't wear down the self-consciousness
which insistently gooses me and every late 20th century
American poet whose work I like.
The sea will not care whether
we lie on the beach or achieve an
immortal work, but let's get busy
and do our best, a gift for each other.

2

Why make art? I think that's the question
every artist ultimately faces, particularly
those who, like poets, make works of art
for which there is little current demand.
Go to the library here, look at the poetry section.
Let's do the town justice; they've got Marianne Moore,
Ted Roethke, even James Merrill,
but who's the poet with the most volumes?
Rod McKuen! And all of them unread.
I know it's an easy target, but
the temptation for the poet is to sneer,
"You half-wits are unworthy of my art,"
alternating with the anguished cry,
"Hey! Won't anybody listen to me?
Don't you care?" And why should they care?
We all, I suppose, have our special daydreams—
I am sitting on a plane next to a
corporate executive. He notices my book of poems.
A conversation ensues. "I've never read poetry,
never understood it." And then I somehow
tell him what it's all about,
give him my blessing and the book I'm reading,
and he deplanes a changed man, so that
when he finally becomes President he has
true wisdom and runs the country
wisely and well, not like the current idiot
who seems determined to leave us a war
as a parting gift. I'll resist a burgeoning
diatribe here and search for a lesser nuisance,
a mosquito which has craftily
penetrated the porch screen and bitten me.
Die, you varmint! I'll also resist
the temptation to make that mosquito a metaphor
for poetry in one for its functions:

namely, to penetrate our defenses, stir us
into uneasiness at times; at others,
to prick us into an awareness of beauty
even here, where it so obviously exists.
I've always distrusted metaphor, while
admiring those who can use it perfectly.
Pound's "In a Station of the Metro"—wow!
(Another idle dream—
if felled in a public place, by a heart attack
or an assassin's bullet, I rouse myself
and gasp those lines as my last words
to the faces crowding around.) Or Cavafy
in that poem where he compares his days
to a row of lighted candles going out
one by one. I have a similar subject:
you know how I always bend over and
pick up a penny that I find in the street.
"It's good luck," I say, and I take that penny
home to my penny jar. Now, there's an image
ripe for the plucking; it can be sliced or pureed,
used in so many dishes. Are the pennies
contemporary manna from heaven?
Symbolic of the allure of consumerism,
so shiny and so addictive? And when the jar is filled
and I roll them up, am I thereby
giving my luck away? Rendering unto Mammon?
The metaphor can be turned in a number of ways,
all so poetic you could just shit.
You'd like that, wouldn't you? You've always had
a weakness for the "poetic," just like your
taste for justifiably obscure novelists.
It's one of the things I love you for,
but it's not the ground of our friendship.
We're not supposed to get along, you know,

you're a Pisces, while I'm a textbook example
of the Gemini. One thing, though,
has linked us. I rarely remember
meeting someone for the first time,
but I remember you. I walked into the museum lobby,
and Bob Gottlieb introduced us.
We talked a little, and somehow I knew
that here was someone who was possessed
by art the way that I was.
Possessed by art—is that a shameful thing
for a man or a woman to admit? To love something
so much that it can crowd out love for people?
It's not a matter of whether I'd save
my daughter or the Mona Lisa from a fire;
the real question is whether I'd give up
the making of art if it meant my daughter's life.
Yes, I would, but it would be like leaping
in front of a car to knock her out of the way,
an honorable form of suicide. But even that's
an overstatement of the question. Would I
give up the making of art, my obsession with it,
if I could thereby be a better father, better husband,
more loving and more concerned? No,
come out of the closet and admit it:
poetry I will not give up.

3

The wind is from the east today,
betokening a change. We walked the beach
this morning, poking the flotsam
and looking for shells. Why be a sculptor
when the sea can make such perfect shapes?
You know why—because the sea also makes
a lot of junk, and it is often the role of the artist
simply to edit, to put a frame around something
whether he made it or not. I was thinking
yesterday of that series of performance art
we saw ten years ago at Midway studios
—remember? That was the time
when Mary Jane Dougherty did the only
completely successful performance piece
I've ever seen. The old "happening"
would have been a better word for it. It was called
"It's About Time," and she set up in each room
an expert who discoursed on time as seen
in his specialty. A physicist with a machine
that could measure a millionth of a second;
a geologist with a film depicting continental drift,
where one second equaled five thousand years;
a psychologist discussing children's
perceptions of time; and so on.
But it was Michael Frank's part that convinced me
that this was indeed art. His contribution
was an explication of Marvell's
"To His Coy Mistress"; you know,
"Had we but world enough and time."
I got to his room last and was listening
when Mary Jane walked in and announced
"Michael Frank, your time is up."
He was in the middle of a point,
and I asked him to continue. He did so,

but as he talked I became aware
that something had changed.
The talk was still quite interesting,
but I realized that it was no longer
a work of art. The artist had said up
a frame for that event and said,
"It's art because I say it is."
And it *was* art, as this is art,
because I say it is. What charms and talismans
we use to keep our courage up
when going on our nerve.
It's art. It's art. Poetry
by force of will.
One moment's lack of faith, and you're sinking,
but faith in what for us? Faith in the belief
that somehow, somewhere, someone will pick up
this book and be moved as we were moved?
Sounds corny, yet it's capable
of touching me to the core. Years ago
I read a poem in some anthology that I
never saw again. It's become my own Lost Chord.
I don't remember the poet; he was
late Victorian. The title
was something like "To Future Poets."
The poet addresses us, saying,
I don't know how things are when you're living,
but you still love moonbeams and candlelight,
you still enjoy wine and roses, and he ends,
"I send my soul through time and space
To greet you. You will understand."

And, damn it, I *do* understand, even
with all my amused condescension for that
Dowsonesque stuff. We go on,
Fayoum mummy painters making our own effigies
so that someone in the future
can pick up the book, and the words will drop away,
and there, looking at him across the gap,
is us, though dead for years.
Art. Kilroy was here. Are they the same?

4

The weather did change yesterday, with rain blowing
over all the windows. Stuck inside,
I read the children stories, played Go Fish,
and found myself silently nagged. No nanny,
and no time to write. I suppose it's fair
we men get a taste of what unmonied women
who want to write have to put up with,
but I don't think it leads to greater understanding,
it just spreads the frustration around.
Naomi's in college now and hasn't
lived with you for years, anyway,
so you've got the time to make art.
I say that I envy you, knowing fill well
that I'm lazy, fart off many opportunities to write,
despite that stern conscience my
parents bequeathed to me along with
blue eyes and a big nose. Roberta told me,
"Your conscience never stopped you from doing anything;
it just makes you feel guilty about it." What a
worthless emotion guilt is. I used to think it was a
useful goad, but I don't anymore. I didn't know then
that guilt is a cumulative thing. It begins
as a sharp corner in your backpack, urging you
to get on to the next clearing fast and take care of it.
But each offense, each betrayal adds its bit,
and the pack weighs more and more until
you simply lie there beneath the load.
I think that's one appeal the sea has
for me. Others may point to it
as agent of destruction, whether
Plato on Atlantis or Pat Boone's immortal
"Love Letters in the Sand," but
it's comforting to walk the beach
early in the morning and find

the sand swept clean for the new day,
all our grotesqueries touched
by Shakespeare's sea change.
That piece of electric cable we found this morning—
marvelous! Like a giant sea worm's tube.
In these days of oil spills and atomic radiation,
I don't kid myself that the sea's eternal
or that it can always heal
itself and me, but if there is hope, if we
can somehow avoid giving in to the
stupidity of ourselves and others, perhaps
a poet in two hundred years
can walk this beach and understand this poem.
If he's like you and me, he will,
and he'll incorporate this poem into all
the other baggage he carries with him, thinking,
"The wind is from the east today, like in that
old poem I read once. I'm having trouble
writing here, just like in Auden's 'Pleasure
Island.' Surely that's the best poem
ever written about the beach. Ouch!
My foot's still sore where I stepped on that shell
while wading yesterday. Yes,
the bottom of the sea *is* cruel. Hmm.
Could I work that in somewhere? Wait,
I'm going to stop all these allusions, going to simply
sit here and experience the scene
in all its hereness, or is it
thereness? Ah, sky! Sea! Sand!
And dunes! And, uh, sky! And . . ."
We'll leave him there, heroically struggling
with his true nature.

5

A couple of days have gone by. You've left
already, and we leave tomorrow. Buzz,
I enjoyed having you here, enjoyed
gossiping about the artworld,
going to movies, working the jigsaw
puzzle. We looked through the telescope
at Jupiter and Saturn; since you've gone,
Roberta and I found the Andromeda Galaxy.
I love it here, although, being plains-bred,
I find it like taking a second wife,
and a foreigner at that. I try
to fit my responses to a new other
who can never be completely known.
Like the Andromeda Galaxy, the sea
ignores me and goes on
mumbling the beach at the foot of the hill.
Two images come to mind.
The first if of Keats, sitting by the shore
and seeing, as he wrote to Reynolds,
"Too far into the sea, where every maw
The greater on the less feeds evermore."
It can never seem fully friendly to me,
even though I've quieted my imagination
and no longer believe there's a shark out there
with my name on it. Can we ever
relax and know that we're part of nature?
Sitting here in comfort, I think it possible,
but what if I were in the fix of Pip,
my second image, in *Moby Dick*,
abandoned and floating in the middle
of the ocean? Could I, instead of cracking up,
surrender to the power, feel myself
part of the system about to
swallow me? An admirable goal, but

not unlike the human sacrifice who does a
triple gainer on her way into the mouth
of the volcano. I'll leave the sea
and drag myself back to New York, bringing
this with me. I hope, going over it
in the noise and fug of the city, I can
bear it without loathing. I won't edit much;
whatever its faults, it's a part of my life
now, in this place. One last snapshot:
the other night, driving back from town,
Roberta and I saw a fox. A friend
tells us that in the Orient having a fox
cross one's path is an omen of good fortune.
Oh, please, god or goddess who sent the red one,
I shamelessly ask for a lot more good luck
on top of that which I've frittered away.
I'll take money, fame, success in love,
whatever you've got that's good. And with a fresh
deposit into my account, I'd like
to transfer some to my best friend Buzz:
may he have enough time
to fulfil his gift, may he recognize
his truth and not hate it, and when
the years wash over his work, may it still,
miraculously, stay.

III

Upon a Time

The Ogre

An ogre wore a jewel of great repute,
but took no pleasure in it, could not recall
how it was come by, legacy or loot,
and would but for its worth have let it fall.
He had enough to carry as it was—
his foul familiars: a grinning rat
nuzzled his scabby cheeks, tarantulas
slept in his pockets, snakes coiled round his hat.
A princess passed. "Take care of this for me,"
the ogre begged, "And wear it as your own."
Struck by its gleam, she knelt, and on her breast
the ogre hung it.
Years went by. The stone
grew into millstone, slowly crushed her. See
the ogre stroke the spider on his chest.

The Saint

Each morning brought the ravens to his rock
bearing his daily bread. He ate but half;
half-starved, he gave the other to his flock
of wandering lepers. Once he heard a laugh
while at such charity, but could not tell
whom he amused. No sound of hovering wing
competed with the lepers' warning bell.
His holiness increased. The jeering gang
of imps had long departed. As he prayed
one day he could not but admire the choice
stigmata on his hands. His heart was glad.
From behind, there came a soft, old, mocking voice:
"Though I should give my body to be burned,
yet have not love . . ." He clenched his fists and turned.

The Soldier

Disarmed, defrauded of his pay, unhorsed,
the shabby soldier tramped the road for home,
his wiles his weapons now, a beggar forced
in stingy towns to conjure soup from stone.
Sometimes he found companions for his needs
—Wind-Maker, Light-Foot, Sharp-Eyes, Carry-Load—
and with their help did princess-winning deeds,
yet in the end his boots resumed the road.
No aged parent waited, and no wife
kept warm the marriage bed. If former life
gave orders for his march and made him deaf
to silken pleading, no one knew. The span
of swordpoint's arc held room for only one:
tighten the shako's chinstrap and march on.

The Devil's Grandmother

With eyes as old and black as coal, she bent
over the sleeping head upon her lap
as if to kill his lice. There came the scent
of human flesh upon his breath. In sleep
his horny hands convulsed, longing to rend
the limbs of sinners. Blood-red in the glare,
the adamantine walls of Hell curved round
and echoed when she plucked the golden hair.

He, who knew of toad at fountain's heart
and mouse at root of tree, how had he missed
the trembling boy now hidden in her skirt,
for whom the Devil's hair fulfilled a quest?
Her trick? His inattention? Or a crude,
unspoken compact, evil warding good?

The Knight

I

The sun beat down. There rose a sickening smell
from rocks stained white with droppings. Underfoot,
a helmet like a broken mussel shell
went rattling from his horse's hoof. The sweat
that trickled down his nose could not be wiped
away with an iron-clad finger, and the flea
at work beneath his mail could not be stopped.
No breeze brought sound of the now-distant sea.

His past and future lives lay in a cove
an hour behind. They and his groom would wait
three days at most, then past and groom would leave
and future turn to rumors of his fate.
The horse reared. As he landed on his back,
a weathered skull rolled grinning to his cheek.

II

He woke as from a nightmare, but the dream
continued into waking. Like a bride,
the loathsome monster's crudely hacked-off arm,
untouched by flies, lay dozing at his side.
His dented armor grated on a stone
as he rolled to struggle upright with a curse.
No sword could serve him for a makeshift cane:
the shattered blade lay back by his dead horse.

The trail of blood was black. How long had he
lain senseless? Was the ship about to sail?
He grasped a claw and felt malignancy
burn cold as frost through armor. Like a tail,
his trophy smeared his track. Another fall.
His legs refused to hobble. He would crawl.

The Woodsman

A trampled fern, the echoes of a horn,
give hint of someone near, yet when he comes,
he still surprises, breaking in to warn,
recount, or rescue, many-guised—sometimes
a wide-eyed yokel stammering what he's seen
(the bird with golden plumage, the she-bear
suckling a human cub), sometimes a man
silent and grim in hunter's green and fur,
who kills the wolf. The plot turned on its course,
he disappears and does not come again.
The goose-girl weds a prince, the wicked nurse
is punished; all are changed, except the one
who chops his wood or chases wonted game,
unknowing as the stone that turned a stream.

The Queen

Artless, she gives away what I possess
through art alone now. Young and fair, I won
the king, her father, on whose white-haired breast
I lay each night, my eyes cat-open. Soon
he lay in state. None has slept at my side
for two nights running since. The act of love
sends all its swollen pleasure to my pride,
pleasure that lies in knowing I can give
or take away such pleasure. All men's eyes
but served for mirrors once. This budding flirt
has tarnished them. Huntsman, bring me her heart;
I'll eat it. Queens should never end their days
as crones. I'll make me sole desire again,
then let all beauty die with me, amen.

The Fool

A merchant had a fat wife *(Indicate
her girth.)* who liked her nightly mug of beer.
(Steal someone's drink and gulp it.) Full of cheer
the lady was, sitting before a plate
of tripe with caraway. *(They start to laugh
as you relieve a lackey of his tray
and demonstrate her gorging.)* Well, one day,
*(Speak while you're eating. You must get enough
to fill your belly.)* passing a door she heard
her handmaid, crying, "Master! Now! Oh, now!"
*(They slap their thighs, knowing whose mistress' voice
you imitate. He grips his pommel. How
had you known that? He'll have you beaten. Cease
the story; raise your jester's wand.)* En garde.

The Lord

The palace dogs no longer deigned to sniff
the mummied trophy hanging on the wall
their sires had growled at. Youth now heard the tale
and smiled politely. Taciturn and stiff,
nursing his pain, he sat at meals, his chair
the rock on which the dinner chatter broke.
As servants cleared, he rose, turning his back
on guests awaiting fool and troubadour.

The battlement was cold, and yet he stood
as if on guard, hands crossed against the chill,
echoing those of her who rested now
transposed to limestone in the crypt below.
The sun had gone. He watched the evening clouds
forming their ranks to fight on the last red hill.

IV

Hay Fever

Here I sit, eyes overflowing, ears clogged,
nose bursting like a dam when I bend over,
reminding myself that Goethe composed while seasick
and while playing the lover.

Amour and *mal de mer,* puissant conditions
that overwhelm our everyday defenses
(which might assist a poet—see Rimbaud's
derangement of all senses)

have settings on Verona balconies
in moonlight or on rocking, wave-washed decks
which lend exotic gloss to unromantic
physical facts.

Hay fever, on the other hand, stays home,
confronts its pained reflection clutching a bottle
of antihistamines. Its abject woes
are never fatal.

Here I sit, working with what I have.
Peevish self-hatred shoves aside self-pity,
sneering *"Goethe? Rimbaud?* You poetic
Walter Mitty!"

Begone, self-hatred. Take self-pity with you.
Hay fever, leave me for another year.
And you, clownish, toad-eating alter-ego,
disappear.

Let pen scratch, fingers drum, let all the work
of literary harvestide begin,
so that the fruit of this September night
be gathered in.

Instructions

Catch the sluicings,
swirl the pan,
bite to test—
disgust, disgust.

The Water Lily

Sun, incessant sun, would be its wish,
if it could wish, resplendent as it rocks
upon the gentle ripples. Languid fish
meander through its shadow. From the docks
the mothers call their children back to shore,
an echoing irrelevance, no more.
The water lily rides the lake.

The struggles for survival fought below,
each hungry lunge and desperate retreat,
are nothing to it as it crests the slow,
subsiding slipstream of a distant boat.
A frog may shelter on its floating pad
or be devoured, neither good nor bad.
The water lily rides the lake.

The damselfly nymph crawling from the depths
along its swaying, green umbilicus
does not disturb the lily. It accepts
the pollinating beetle's clumsy kiss
with like indifference. In pelting squall,
it curls into a tight, protective ball.
The water lily rides the lake.

The shimmering reflections of high noon
surround the lily, seeming to construct
a temple for itself, itself alone.
One day its selfish beauty may be plucked
by a careless, arbitrary hand, but now,
in this unblinking, everlasting now,
the water lily rides the lake.

Judgment

Many are dead, some aborted mute,
others quietly strangled when they lied.
The survivors, huddled around his fire,
bear his features, speak
with the cadence of discipline.
They know their own. Each newcomer is eyed,
ripe for denunciation.

But what of this wild-eyed one,
stumbled into the firelit circle?
Do they risk a patsy's ridicule
and kneel as to a prophet?
Do they claw for stones to hurl?

Who put that tongue in its mouth?

Greene County

Upstate New York, writers' well-traveled country:
another writer walks a country lane,
sniffing the air, swatting at flies. A Sunday
peace hangs over all. The evening rain

is still two hours away. My eye is caught
by yellows, whites, and purples—all the life
that riots in the bar ditch at my foot.
Seen from a car, with nothing but a brief

sideways glance, a bushel of confetti
tossed by the road, but viewed from close at hand,
one yellow splits into three flowers—a pretty
pineapple-shaped affair, a long-stemmed fan

dividing into five inverted hearts,
each with a smaller mussel shell below,
and a deep, five-pointed star that hugs the dirt
with round-leafed runners. But I do not know

their names and cannot give them names myself
—I am no Adam, and this isn't Eden—
and, lacking names, the flowers stay but half-
perceived, oddly. It seems the classic Western

movie cliché applies here, where the old
cowpuncher meets a stranger and demands,
"What's your handle, Pardner?" To take hold
requires a handle. Namelessness withstands

all efforts made to apprehend it. We
can't think what we can't say. Could it be true
we can't see what we cannot name? The bee
with her instinctive knowledge fumbling through

this blossom is responding to a shape,
a smell, a color, signifying food.
A stimulus and a response—no gap
between perception and the understood.

But "I am Two with Nature." Woody's quip
hits home. Our school-taught, scientific means
serve us but poorly. How can we sum up
without encoded knowledge in the genes?

Back from my walk, I scan this country home's
bookshelves for a field guide which has full-
color illustrations, gives the names
both Latin and familiar, and details

the virtues of each pod and tender shoot,
will say a poultice of the cat-tail's fur
can ease the chicken pox, or that its root
was used by fullers, whatever fullers were.

The volume found, a casual study yields
a plethora of names, the legacy
of Indian killers, farmers in their fields,
and country parsons on an idle day.

Their souls infused with God and apple brandy,
they broke and named the land with plow and axe,
a taste for metaphor, and an ear for the spondee—
Harebell. Cowbane. Sneezeweed. Skullcap. Toadflax.

Names stiff upon the tongue, archaic as
the rusted iron contraptions seen behind
the wreckage of a barn, drowning in grass.
Manmade and natural there lie intertwined,

almost at peace, unlike this room where fact
and recollection war, imperiling
a hesitant attempt in retrospect
to pair a picture with a living thing.

The few that match in memory will become
additions to the dog-eared mental chart
called, "Things I Think I Know"—a plant and name,
a place, a world, my own divided heart.

V

Mother and Son

Kitchen, Night

Hands that hit are washing hair.
The child lies on a towel, stretched
along the counter's length. No fear
invades the moment as, untouched

except in love, his head lolls back,
accepting their solicitude.
One rests across his brow to block
his eyes from the soapy, scented flood.

The other hand directs the spray,
playing it across his skull.
The knotted anger of the day
dissolves into a basinful

of winking bubbles. Overhead,
the kitchen clock ticks on its wall
pulsing with their common blood,
 its face, like hers, invisible.

His backside bears the memory
of silent fury, but at bath
the hands caress him. How is he
to understand which touch is truth?

Taller, unwilling to believe
that both are truth, he turns away
the hands' feckless attempts at love,
keeping her remorse at bay.

Anger still arises, but
the blows are feebler now, almost
pro forma. With her mind's retreat,
love and anger both are lost.

Today the hands play with a doll,
clap to the nurse's music, help
to speak. Unoccupied, they will
arrange and rearrange themselves.

The child, now bald and middle-aged,
carries the anger for them both,
striving to keep it safely caged,
but feels it growl at evening bath

when baffled animosity
and love begin together their
involuntary inventory:
Night. Sweet water. Hands. Hair.

Letters from Connie

Texas, 1950s

So good to get your letter. I am busy
preparing for my sketching class. We practice
drawing the figure from all angles. Art
and children—two hard masters. I also made
an abstract piece. Leon said it made him sick
to see me waste my skill on such a thing.

Another year already gone! Something
always comes up. It's been extremely busy;
both children and the baby have been sick.
Leon has been working at his practice
so many hours, the other doctors made
him partner. Healing truly is an art.

Enclosed is a clipping about the local art
fair, where I won first prize, a thing
that's been eclipsed by bigger news: we've made
another baby. You should see the busy-
bodies arch their eyebrows, asking if practice
makes perfect. Four, they think, is sick.

A hard delivery. Then I was feeling sick
not three months later. Oops. It took no art
to diagnose: another baby. Practice
patience, I tell myself. If anything
can teach me, this will. Seeing me so busy,
Leon, bless him, hired a colored maid.

I've been remiss, not writing, but dismayed,
I vow to write more often. (Please don't sic
the dogs on me!) Girl Scouts have kept me busy.
I help the kids with projects, turn my art
supplies to other uses, try for nothing
too difficult. My hand is out of practice.

Ballet, the supermarket, baseball practice—
I don't know where I am, sometimes. I made
a bas-relief in clay of each child, something
for Leon's office. Now the waiting sick
can see my children, captured in my art.
I would have done more, but I've been too busy.

* * *

Each year I grew more practiced in the art
of self-effacement. Lovesick for a thing
denied, I made a life of staying busy.

Alzheimer's

Each day my mother in her wheelchair bends
a hair's breadth closer to a fetal pose.
Her staring eyes are vacant, and her hands
fold like a baby's onto nothing. Nose
to nose, cajoling, my sad father keeps
performing love's last duty twice a day:
to hold her death at bay
by spooning mush through her indifferent lips,

Over the last eight years they said goodbye,
my siblings, in word or look when they could feel
contact was being made. Self-exiled, I
waited until the nursing home to kneel,
whisper I loved her, thank her for the art
within me, kiss, and give her leave to go.
Did she even know?
Or was I simply easing my own hurt?

Unknowing, unresponsive, Mother is now
a vessel into which we pour our love,
my brother says, determined to allow
our mother her condition. Can he have
it both ways, believing this, not hearing any
paradox or echo of despair
in his daily prayer:
"Dear Lord, today please take your servant Connie"?

Each day the features in my mirror grow
more like my father's. I may look like him,
but I'm my mother's son. How well I knew
the turnings of her mind. I have her grim
survival skills, her bottled anger—pain
transfixed by art—her bourgeois sense of fashion,
her mild depression.
Do I also have the dry rot in my brain?

Mother would have called her fate God's will,
immutable as any moral law.
I sneer at that, intending to rebel,
take arms against a sea, etcetera,
and exit in possession of my mind.
The rub: if I can tell what's going on,
it's too soon,
but when I can't, all choice comes to an end.

Should I appoint a guardian for my brain?
No family member but some friend who, seeing
me almost gone, would speak to the remaining
fragment of myself, thoughtfully weighing
my poor head in his hands, stroking my brow
as if to diagram the missing part,
then press my heart:
"If you still want to do it, do it now."

And then what? Would I rush off straightaway,
hoping to get to gun or pills before
the fog came down forever? No delay,
or find myself befuddled in my chair,
staring at a note, its text obscure
as words shouted across a windy gulf:
"Remember! Kill yourself!"
until it falls unnoticed to the floor.

Mother has no such worries as she sits
oblivious to the others, to the aide
who washes her or changes dirty sheets.
That is, I hope her intellect has faded
with the rest of her. I hope there is no clash
of mind with body struggling to die,
no silent cry
buried alive in unresponding flesh.

Perhaps my fears are baseless, perhaps Mother
has pleasant dreams; perhaps she splashes in
that river she desired, where we shall gather,
singing our hallelujahs, but within
her eyes the lack of light befits a tale,
far older, of a dark and sullen stream.
Across it come no gleam
of welcoming lamp or last wave of farewell.

Inheritance

"You sounded just like your mother when you said that."
—My wife, in conversation

Her last two years, she did not speak,
then death sealed fast her lips, and fire
consumed the lips completely. What
could still today remain of her,
whose ashes go to ground beneath
a dusty Texas family plot?

Her genes, of course, passed down, survive.
I see them in the wary smile
my niece presents. They hold their place
within my daughter's deep-set eyes
and delicately sculpt the chin
upon her new great-grandchild's face.

Yet more, incredibly, survived,
for when the elemental stuff
that formed the individual
went back into the melting pot,
a part of her remained alive,
escaping from its human cell.

Evanescent as a breath,
a voice first heard *in utero*
outlived its owner to become
a lasting presence in my speech,
transformed, yet recognizable,
in strictest sense, my mother tongue.

VI

Jim Brodey

The Whitney, in a show last month
displayed in an expensive mat
a strip of coin-booth photographs
by Andy Warhol. In them sat

a young man in the Sunday suit
and necktie he would soon discard:
prize-winning poet, up-and-comer,
darling of the *avant-garde,*

Jim Brodey, with his hair still short.
laughed for the camera, quite at ease
while entering art history.
(Perhaps the artist muttered, "Cheese.")

One of the Lower East Side crew,
Jim gave the New York School a poke
with funny yet hermetic verse
—the man who out-Koched Kenneth Koch—

and won himself inclusion in
the Random House *Anthology
of New York Poets,* studbook of
the hipster aristocracy.

I met him eight years after that
at Saint Mark's Church. My reading there
filled half the seats. I read the last
well-crafted poem and sought my chair

acknowledging polite applause,
thanking the host, exchanging hugs
with my invited audience
when he stood up. Was he on drugs?

He had been sitting in the back.
Now, blocking my way without a fuss,
he gave his name and then remarked,
as if to state the obvious,

"I wanted to see what you looked like,"
What did *that* mean? Defensiveness
prevented any glib response
as silently I tried to guess

if he was simply greeting me,
or was it an attempt to bait
the square he must have thought I was?
But he did not elaborate.

The cryptic utterance left me
nonplussed. I don't know what I said
and can't recall if we shook hands.
A few years later, he was dead.

The supercharged, ecstatic high
Jim courted in his poetry
turned vampire, bit him, and began
to feed on his vitality.

Poète maudit, a classic case
with modern ways to jolt the brain:
instead of absinthe, LSD,
amphetamines, then crack cocaine.

Addiction took its course until
the visitor to Tompkins Square
might see, among the usual drunks,
a homeless poet sitting there.

Then he was gone. The poet whom
that hungry Muse adores dies young,
some yellowed pages and his gift
among her crumbling trophies hung.

Today there is a faint but real
survivor's guilt as I sit here
with mailings from AARP
and catalogs for garden gear.

Silly, of course. Our countrymen
indulge their taste for lighter fare
and want no truck with poetry,
outré or *retardataire*.

Yet poems keep our collective heart
alive as nothing else can do,
at length reshape degraded speech
and make the ancient feelings new.

Poets share this human duty,
writing gray-haired or dying young.
A small salute, Jim, brother poet:
live on in the altered tongue.

Ohrwurm

Something is always playing. In my waking hours
and, for all I know, the sleeping ones as well,
non-stop music courses through my brain
just below the level of conscious thought.
American Songbook, teeny-bopper tripe,
Whatever—unbidden, a song is always there.
This morning's absent-minded humming may
have had its source in a song heard yesterday
on the radio, but sometimes a mysterious finger
scrolls down a list of half-remembered songs
and presses "Play." Most often, songs will come
and go without their even registering
to consciousness, but sometimes—what sometimes!—
the volume gets cranked up, and a single song
can play itself without pause for days on end.
"Ear Worm," the Germans call it, that condition
when, like a virus invading a healthy cell,
a song embeds itself and won't let go.

Desperate in such cases, I often try
to light a backfire, hoping that two songs
will burn each other out. The other song
can vary. Bubble-gum fare with a hook can work,
though the opening bars of Brahms' Fourth Symphony
have done the trick at times. When the scheme succeeds,
the mind cannot hold on to both songs at once.
Some melody insinuates itself
in the dead space, and the mind gets back to normal,
wondering how it could have been shanghaied.
Emotions rise and fall, likes and dislikes
assert themselves, and the person I call "me"
resumes his daily life but now is chastened
by a fretting that he doesn't own himself.
Who makes the basic choices if not "me"?
Who picks the melody to which "I" dances?

Valhalla

I tossed the magazine aside, half-read,
and looked to see what station we had reached
on Metro-North. "Valhalla," the sign said.
The setting sun's defiant sally breached
the line of trees beyond the graves that lay
beside the tracks, containing baptized flocks
whose faith assures them on the final day
a call to rise less grim than Ragnarok's.

I wonder, did the shudder of our wheels
run like a current through the heads and heels
of all those dead who lie beneath the saintly
ground the cemetery wall encloses,
causing gold charms on wrists to tinkle faintly
and spectacles to vibrate on dead noses?

Saint Johnsbury

In a land of mountains and grazing cows, where even
the Interstate qualifies as a scenic route,
a modest ramp brings you down to a parade
of oaks and maples fronting Victorian houses.
Vermont Public Radio's heroin warning
goes half-heard, while your eyes caress
the smartly tuckpointed brickwork and the porches
flaunting their freshly painted gingerbread.
There is money here. Yet on Main Street,
whose stores once offered wares to doctors and bankers
as well as to farmers and journeymen, wares
whose names—dry goods, sundries—mean nothing now,
the shops today seem all but abandoned and sad.
When not vacant, their flyspecked windows offer
TV repair and artificial flowers.
Shop names share space with placards for food pantries
and hotlines for domestic violence.
Whippet-thin young men amble the sidewalks
in boots, shorts, sleeveless shirts, and baseball caps
enroute to a day labor job or a drug connection.
The working class elderly with their canes are stout,
victims of the cheap carbohydrates
that form their diets. On the village green,
a banner on the gazebo announces a concert
tomorrow, and a rusted cannon watches over
a cenotaph bearing the names of eighty men
who marched south to the War and never returned.
How did one small town find all those soldiers?
Most no doubt were mourned, though for some homes
the deaths down South may have ended violence
in kitchens and bedrooms. The small farms
most soldiers came from are gone, except for those
of back-to-the-land young people or gentleman farmers.
Only large farms can survive in the general market.

Between thrift shop and automotive supply,
a former post office, now with a patio,
umbrellas, and tables houses a restaurant
targeting you and your middle-class peers.
Photos of Tibetan temples line its walls.
The menu identifies the organic farm
from which the meat was sourced, and your server
tells you her name. The virtuous cooking is good.

After lunch, you visit the Athenaeum,
the century-old endowment of Horace Fairbanks,
a local magnate. Imposing in its mass
it stands, a mighty fortress proclaiming its faith
in two thousand years of culture, its very name
invoking the ancient city of philosophers
and poets, ignoring the demagogues and slaves.
In the vestibule, thumbtacked flyers proclaim
lectures, twelve-step groups, and farmer's markets.
Hanging among them is a framed broadside:
"The Fly" by Galway Kinnell, who read here once.
Inside, ornate parquetry, old-fashioned sconces,
and circular stairways to upper galleries
now off-limits to the public. The reachable shelves
must hold as many DVDs as books.
At the end of the Fiction Room, a pair of doors
open into a gallery where you are gobsmacked
by Albert Bierstadt's *Domes of the Yosemite,*
a wall-filling monument to the sublime.
Compared to this immense recruiting poster
for Westward Expansion and the Course of Empire,
the rest of the collection seems staid and quaint,
the kind of works a provincial robber baron
would acquire—full-sized copies of Old Masters
interspersed with works by the second generation
of the Hudson River School, friends of their patron.

The bourgeois thirst for edifying culture
which found an incarnation here continues
undiluted to this day. Unwitting
novitiates, young people read their books
beneath the murals in the children's room.
Hiawatha, Heidi and Hans Brinker,
instead of saints, are tutelary spirits
of the place, and yet this cluttered room contains
whispers of something once considered sacred
to higher beings than ourselves or, rather,
ourselves as something more than creatures. Here,
alone and yet with others, children draw
communal breath, enroll in a fellowship
greater than themselves, one not to be found
in solitary gazing at a screen.
Outside, the plague, whatever it is called
this time—bubonic, HIV—pursues
its victims endlessly, and violence
goes on, directed or at random, as
it ever has, but here within these walls
the voices of our forebears are absorbed
and for another day the word made flesh.

The Toadstone

Sweet are the uses of adversity;
Which, like the toad, ugly and venomous,
Wears yet a precious jewel in his head.
—Duke Senior, *As You Like It*

Why believe that fable? Any fool
Could easily disprove it with a knife,
this idea that a therapeutic stone
having the potency to save a life

could lie within the compass of a toad's
bewarted head, the stone an antidote
for poison, epilepsy—amulet,
an angel in a dull and ragged coat.

Granted, there were things called toadstones, but
no witnesses attested to their birth.
No matter, those were times when unicorns
and manticores and suchlike walked the earth.

Still, someone must have sought them for himself,
collected toads and killed them, stained his hands
with toad's blood, finding nothing but the brains
of those unfortunate amphibians.

Yet no one told the truth. How many years
until such science was debunked at last?
Ten centuries, at least, elapsed while men
repeated superstitions of the past.

Today the stone, now labelled bufonite,
is known the tooth from a Jurassic fish
long fossilized, its sole significance
as emblem of mankind's eternal wish

for good somehow from evil, joy from tears,
for meaning in a tragedy, to find
the silver lining in the cloud, the boon,
the prayer answered, seen with eyes once blind.

Too Hot Not to Cool Down

You Take My Breath Away. You Can't Change That.
You Always Make Me Smile. You Hung the Moon.
I'll Make You Mine. I Want to Be Your Last.
I Dreamed a Dream. I Long to See You Soon.
You Make Me Feel Brand New. You Set Me Free.
I Feel Love. I Want to Hold Your Hand
You Make It Feel Like Christmas. You and Me.
I Won't Let Go. I Wanna Be Your Man.

You've Lost That Loving Feeling. You're So Vain.
You Don't Send Me Flowers Anymore.
I'm a Fool to Want You. I Can't Stand the Rain.
I Don't Want to Hear It Anymore.
You Think You Know Somebody. You Never Know.
I Should Have Known Better. I Can't Let Go.

Dry

> *...the dryness of his last years, which he so regretted.*
> —Anthony Thwaite on Philip Larkin

Women go dry; men can't get it up,
the spirit willing but the flesh too weak.
Their bodies differ, yet in poetry
there's neither male nor female, Jew nor Greek.

Poets who have dried up see themselves
as empty-headed fools, figures of fun,
or pitiful hermaphrodites in whom
sterility and impotence are one.

Recognition of this altered state
comes slowly. Has our passion left us flat?
No messenger from Eros or the Muse
will tell us that the last time was just that.

Recent photos show us double-chinned
and slack, or pinched and rawboned, stooped with age.
Time at the desk yields only fits and starts
or else the pathos of an empty page.

Inevitably, memory recalls
the time before our gift began to wane.
The pool was overflowing and the act
no sooner finished than begun again.

Wisdom is the trade-off, so we like
to tell ourselves, for youth's exuberance,
a wry corrective to those heady years
we thought ourselves the Muse's fancy pants.

But wisdom brings the knowledge that we fail
so often, and it dogs us as we weigh
the latest effort, fearing to discover
that hours of work have ended in cliché.

A stately silence seems more dignified.
Better forget the poems we have penned
than toss another book onto that pile
of which, the Preacher says, there is no end.

Congealing from the leavings of self-doubt,
what surfaced as a vague disquiet hardens
into a certitude the wisest course
may simply be to cultivate our gardens.

And yet the only garden that we want
grew long ago. Desires wandered loose
as sporting panthers. Love rolled on its back,
while fruit splitting from ripeness dripped its juice,

and we were up for everything. Human,
we shared creation's work. Each animal
came frisking towards us, yearning for the name
that we alone could give. The act was all.

Then something happened, and we found ourselves
exiles in a dusty land with but
our hunger and the memory of a scent
that lingered outside after the gate was shut.

The Old Believers

A beach, but not of the holiday variety,
with perhaps a wall or two of a blasted building,
something they had seen as GI's two years earlier
or simply clipped from any news magazine.
A rag on a makeshift pole, raised in signal
or as flag of surrender by one no longer there.
No sun, a low and ominous gray sky.
No dune rose, cypress tree, sea lavender,
but only sea wrack and some blackened driftwood.

The rags in their hands as they painted these, rubbed out,
and painted again, the acrid fumes of cordite
replaced by the piney smell of turpentine.
If dreams of corpse-strewn atolls seen through smoke
or broken bombers going down in flames
haunted their sleep, the haze of their waking hours
was the smoke of a burning cigarette forgotten
in the lips or tossed in a dirty coffee cup
while they struggled with an image for a world
never again to live without the fear
of the new bomb that could wipe out everything.
The Age of Anxiety—Auden had proclaimed it—
how else to depict it but as ruin and wreckage
inhabited by cowering survivors,
their eyes as empty as the wasteland stretching
into apocalyptic nothingness?

Yet something was not right. Their old-world angst
seemed out of place in rude America.
Paris was cheap, since the dollar was almighty.
Perhaps they should do as previous generations
of Americans had done—go there to paint,
starve in romantic garrets, drink at the Dôme—
until their veterans' benefits ran out.

So they packed their bags, sublet their studios,
and caught the eastbound boats, not noticing
the future was with those who stayed behind,
veterans of the W.P.A.,
the Waldorf Cafeteria, and the Cedar Bar,
who took the age and its attendant chaos
not for enemy but as partner in a dance,
careening, full of risk, and oddly joyful.

While they were gone, their world would be destroyed,
not by a bomb but by Pollock and de Kooning.
After a year or two, they straggled home.
Most tried to find a place in the new order,
and soon picked up the fashionable lingo,
making their abstract art by means of a method
already congealing into formula.

Some, however, stubbornly refused
any accommodation, would not give up
hard-won technique. Instead, they left the city
to make their stands on provincial campuses.
Ignored by the art world press, their shows were held
in student union buildings or outside
faculty lounges, their only followers
well-scrubbed faces wanting a good grade.

Their works were given to local museums,
halfheartedly accepted and soon buried
in basement storage racks where they awaited
the new eyes of a later generation,
fresh-minted curators who viewed the past
not as a simple tale of evolution,
each movement pushing the previous to extinction,
but rather as one big artistic grab-bag.

Rooting through the racks, they found these paintings,
artifacts from another age, and like
the Australian naturalist who first discovered
a platypus egg, paused to stare at something
that should not be and yet was somehow there.

Today those works, unheralded, begin
to sprout upon museum walls, bizarre
night-blooming plants in once-familiar gardens.
As blossoms call to destined pollinators,
sometimes an odd, unfashionable painting
survives as if by fate to find the eyes
able to see it truly. History,
artistic reputation, all such things
become irrelevant, and there remain
only recognition and a fragile
resting place within a beating heart.

Mottes

> motte: *n. dialect*: a copse or small stand of trees on a prairie

They seem almost to float upon the land,
dark ships upon a brown and rolling ocean;
this one crests the low wave of a rise,
that one founders in a gulley's trough.

Driving past, we notice them and wonder
why here, not there? What stone, dropped by a glacier,
served as a reef to snag that one? And here,
what cranny caught and held the floating seed?

Around them, furrowed earth gives evidence
that farmers clear and till. Why were these spared?
Was this small patch too marshy, or did ploughshares
break upon a rock too big to move?

For whatever reason, they survived.
An inventory of their native fauna—
field mice, a nesting crow, the usual spiders
spinning their webs for flies—would disappoint.

Our need is for exotic denizens:
within this shade, in our imaginations,
mountain lions snarl as they survey us,
fugitives in leg irons wait for nightfall.

Such fancies have no risk of being disproved,
for we will never stop the car, have clothing
torn by the fence's barbs, and stumble through
a muddy field to a prosaic find.

We leave the mottes inviolate as those groves
scattered across our brains, havens from which
strange beings break into our dreams, envoys
from the darkness we suspect is our true home.

A Bestiary

The BUM STEER
shouldn't really be here,
and yet, transposed to animal,
charmingly louche it rambles, *toujours gai,*
oblivious to the butcher's block until
it meets an end decidedly not Grade-A:
on a bed of soggy toast, its juices mingle
in an Army dish called Shit on Shingle.

The CAT'S PAW
breaks the law
or does a dirty deed for someone else.
Unwitting or unwilling, he's a tool.
The master hides behind events unfolding
and pays the piper for his dancing fool
who discovers that his partner in the waltz
is the empty bag he finds himself left holding.

The DOGSBODY,
is no hot toddy,
or grog (though it belongs to the Royal Navy),
no rack of lamb with gravy,
but a boiled pudding of dried eggs and peas
and also, as we hear him puff and wheeze,
the name of the lowly stiff who bears the brunt
of the kind of work that's often labeled "grunt."

The JUDAS GOAT
has turned his coat.
Trained in deceit, he leads the herd to slaughter.
Despise him, preach what good men ought or
ought not do, but can you really know,
when death was everywhere and bodies burned,
wanting to live, that you would not have turned
Sonderkommando?

The PIG IN A POKE
is for sale when you're broke,
and it's tempting, although you can't see it.
Your future feels trapped like a cat in a well,
and this lottery ticket could free it.
Any sensible person would scoff at the pig and decry it.
You know that your chance is a snowball's in hell
and you buy it.

The SACRIFICIAL LAMB
does not get to say "I am,"
but is told, "You are."
Politicians wanting war
will cloak ambition in an age-old story:
Dulce et decorum est pro patria mori.
Young people, when you are offered a death called sweet,
resist their call to baa and bleat.

The STALKING HORSE
might as well be a hearse
where birds are concerned, for death walks behind it.
The hunter takes cover beside its broad flank
and moves ever closer. The birds do not mind it,
ignoring the beast till quick shots take their lives.
What hunters are stalking us, closer than we dare think,
so close they're within us now, waiting to pounce with their
    knives?

Crosses

After the bloodstained wrecks are towed away,
reports are filed, and funerals are held,
we often see, like mushrooms after rain,
these humble roadside crosses springing up
amid the shards of glass and mangled bolts,
white-painted crossbars trussed or tacked together
and garlanded with artificial flowers.

Sometimes a name is daubed across the arms.
More often the dead remain anonymous,
and even with a name, how could we know
the truth of the one who died here, if he was
a faithful husband, loving father of three,
enroute from a demanding late-shift job,
who skidded on an icy patch of road,
or the scapegrace sort with a suspended license
 who called a boozy *See-ya!* to his pals
as the tavern closed and, staggering to his car,
went barreling off, his radio blaring, only
to miss a hairpin turn two miles away?

Irrelevant, to guess at saint or rascal—
somebody loved the dead enough to hazard
stopping on the highway's narrow shoulder
and getting out to plant this small remembrance,
sometimes at serious peril. Near Fahnestock
on the Taconic Parkway, a white cross stands,
well up the rock face into which the driver
must have hurtled headlong. At what risk
did the person who installed it scale the slope,
chancing a fall as cars went whizzing by,
to wedge the cross securely in its crack?

Was he impelled by sentimental feelings
or haunted by the guilt of angry words
that sent the driver out into the dark
to death by accident or suicide?

Unauthorized, untended, they remain,
year after year, as no officious trooper
pulls them up. The orange-vested roadcrews
likewise mow around them as wildflowers
shelter next to faded plastic blooms.
Their white paint peels and weathers, while the facts
that they denote lie elsewhere, weighted down
by marble headstones which, we surely know,
will long outlast these fragile sticks. And yet
as visits from bereaved survivors dwindle
to once or twice a year, and then to never,
headstones, unread by grieving eyes, become
anonymous as tree bark, while these crosses
flicker in the memories of those
who pass them daily, modest evidence
of love and loss, and finally, just love.

Endless Love

Summer of '81, a sweltering night in Brooklyn,
windows open for a non-existent breeze,
Bergen Street dark, except for streetlamps
dappling the sidewalk through the trees,
neon signs touting beer at the corner bodega,
the only place open for two blocks,
whose burglar gates coming down at eleven
would signal the day's true end.

Wife and baby in the next room, I sat by a window,
trying to read, as voices and music
drifted up from the street to our tiny apartment.
No smart phones in those days; music was carried
in boom boxes on shoulders, and now the hit
of the summer, "Endless Love," was on.
As it played, some girls from the projects,
hanging out with their friends in front of the store,
half-jokingly began to sing along
with Diana Ross, *My first love,*
You're every breath that I take,
You're every step I make.
And the boys in the group responded,
clowning at first, but then growing serious
almost in spite of themselves
as they took the part of Lionel Ritchie,
Forever I'll hold you close in my arms
I can't resist your charms.
Back and forth they sang to each other,
while the hackneyed rhymes and schmaltzy arrangement
worked a middling magic, and the group,
sticking their notes with the precision
of a Broadway cast, soared into a unison chorus:
And love, oh love, I'll be a fool for you,
I'm sure. You know I don't mind.

And then it was over. Someone exited the store
with a purchase, weaving his way through the crowd,
and the spell was broken. The group collapsed into giggles,
soon drifting off in twos and threes,
to everyday lives. In the years to come,
some finished high school and went on to jobs,
some married others, some must have drowned
in the waves of crack cocaine and AIDS
about to swamp the neighborhood.
The survivors today, whether widowed and alone
or dandling the latest grandchild on their knees,
do not recall that summer night,
but a gray-haired poet does, and will carry
the memory of it all his days:
a hot night hanging out with friends
in front of a store, the music, the laughter,
the beautiful young bodies, the yearning,
and love. The endless love.

Injun Country

Seated around their campfires two days out
of St. Joe, hopeful, thinking themselves steeled
against all woes to come, they hear the scout
rebuke their confidence, "Keep your eyes peeled—
from here on, we're in Injun country!" Sight
and sound become distrusted, blurred by fear.
The land and its inhabitants unite
to speak as one: We Do Not Want You Here.

The warnings in those Westerns taught a child,
a day will find you drained and plodding, mocked
by brutal sun, your every hope defiled,
while high upon the ridgeline stands a troop
of hostiles, wearing war paint, arrows nocked.
They watch you, stony-faced. And then they swoop.

Carnivore

The hills of Mendocino, that late summer,
lay stretched around us, tawny as the haunches
of a sleeping lion, you said, so much alike,
that if you were to touch them, you would find
their grass as soft as fur, being the same color.
It was the other way around, of course:
the grass was not the color of a lion;
a lion is the color of its grass.
You might have said the hills were like gazelles
and elands, or the shadows zebra-striped.
Protective coloration is the yin
to camouflage's yang, grim predator
and frightened prey matched to each other's hue,
or, rather, both matched to the dry savanna.

The landscape of my boyhood was as flat
as the dusty football field that it surrounded,
where junior-high-school warriors prepared
for Friday's game, something much more than sport,
they told us: it would show what we were made of.
Under the coach's unforgiving eye,
not-quite-men proving our half-baked manhood,
we sucked it up, we shook it off, we played
with pain and showed the world we weren't pansies.
Afterwards, our locker-room bravado
echoed off the steamy shower tiles.
Our towel-popping horseplay was as close
as most of us would get to other boys.
How many of us already feared they might
be what we all purported to despise?
I don't know to this day. Whatever doubts
I had about my masculinity,
I had things easier, since I liked girls,
and my desire to touch their budding breasts
was quite unfeigned.

            A leopard cannot change
its spots, but I changed mine the following year,
trading my football jersey for a skin
more stippled in its hue, with intellect
and any sign of sensitivity
well-camouflaged by deprecating humor.
What was I so afraid of? At the time,
I thought that I was prey, needing protection
from hungry jaws, but now a backward gaze,
if honest, falls upon a line of victims,
whose hearts I clawed, whose helpless cubs I killed.
From mewling whelp, I had grown into rogue male.

Now with the sunshine warm upon my haunch,
my stomach full, I loll on the savanna.
I recognize myself at last. I know
the taste upon my tongue is blood, not grass.

Aubade

The birds are raising happy hell.
—Frederick Eckman

March 1st, 6:00 A.M., a sparrow
starts his racket on the sill
nearby our bed. No subtlety,
but from the start, insistent, shrill,

a one-man-band that soon will grow
as more and more performers come,
approximating music. Things
devolve to an unruly scrum

instead of orchestra, each male
demanding to be soloist
with alternating repertoires—
To rivals, *Beat it! Scram! Get lost,*

and stay the hell away! To females,
Baby, Baby, Baby, please!
The winner struts upon the ledge
as losers scold from nearby trees.

His song will change when a mate is found
and a nest is filled with eggs to brood,
the noise gaining a treble note
as hungry chicks demand their food.

Their lives will be uncertain, tracked
by wily predators that stalk
their daily errands: feral cats,
the ever-lurking Cooper's Hawk,

or else torrential rains may sweep
their nest from off the sill, put paid
to fond parental labors, leaving
scattered twigs with nestlings dead.

For now, however, they are safe,
and every morning, earlier on,
we hear their boast, *Our tiny lives
have made it to another dawn!*

Awakened from a shortened sleep,
as chirps and flutterings begin,
you pull the blanket past your head
to stuff your ears against the din

and groan in protest, *Stupid birds!
Give it a rest!* Oblivious,
they sing their matins heartlessly,
indifferent to plea or curse.

And like the birds', our humble lives
must meet what fate has got in store.
One day, this bed will lie unused;
this home, our place, know us no more.

Across that empty spot will fall
the shadow of a raptor's wing,
but now the morning light breaks forth.
Wake up, my love. Arise and sing.

Crib Song

A faint noise from upstairs—I take a peek
at the monitor. My two-year-old granddaughter,
lying in her crib and still awake,
is singing snatches of a song I taught her.
Not yet asleep, not big enough to climb
out of her prison, does she yearn to wander
off with little Susie in the rhyme
to pick the paw-paws in their patch down yonder?

When the day comes that I lie in some bed
not knowing who I am, my errant brain,
straining at thought, may catch a memory
of Mother singing me the melody
and join in a duet, now comforted
as Susie picks the paw-paws once again.

Voyager

On November 5, 2018, Voyager 2 exited the heliosphere to enter interstellar space, the region between the stars. Scientists predict that it will outlast the earth. (News item)

Unlike a fertilizing sperm
that penetrates the ovum's skin,
transmuting into something new,
Voyager bursts from deep within

the bubble of the heliosphere,
borne outward on a solar wind
and enters an environment
impossible to comprehend,

an empty-yet-not-empty space
described as a hard vacuum
inhabited by lonely atoms.
Hydrogen and helium,

neutrinos, dust, and cosmic rays
make up a plasma thought to be
filled with something called dark matter
shot through with dark energy.

Awaiting each delayed response
from Voyager, the scientists
must race against the probe's lifespan
to answer questions from their lists,

as forty-year-old instruments
will send them data for at most
a decade more until at last
the batteries give up the ghost.

Its scientific mission done,
Voyager will change roles, to be
a hopeful message in a bottle
cast upon a cosmic sea.

Affixed to its exterior,
a gold recording disk includes
in fifty-five Earth languages
the greetings of our multitudes,

our music, classical to pop,
a huge grab-bag of noises filled
with birdsong, crickets, wind, and surf,
the hubbub of our world distilled,

and images of supermarket,
gymnasts, dolphins, the Great Wall,
Jane Goodall with her chimpanzees,
the Golden Gate, the Taj Mahal,

a person with an ice cream cone,
a missile launch, a traffic jam,
plus "How to Get to Planet Earth"
shown by a helpful diagram.

We crammed this data on the disk,
envisioning some far-off day
(if "day" has any meaning there)
an alien spaceship makes its way

between the planets of some system
light years off, its shape and size
in our imaginations not
unlike the *Starship Enterprise*.

Astride the bridge, the bold commander
guides his ship. His scaly skin
is blue, but nonetheless we find him
recognizable as kin.

An indicator starts to ping.
The Second Mate, with puzzled brow,
looks up from his screen. "Commander!
Spacecraft off the starboard bow."

A tractor beam hauls in the object.
Crewmen jostle to perceive,
etched upon the gold, two humans,
naked as Adam and his Eve.

The artist drew us trim and nubile,
no fat paunch or sagging breast.
(Even among space aliens,
our pride demands we look our best.)

The aliens decode the data;
yottabyte computers start
their task to parse the difference
between Chuck Berry and Mozart.

Safe, the probe has missed the time
when, swelling to gigantic mass,
our Sun incinerated Earth,
reducing it to swirling gas.

We hope, despite the odds of crossing
paths in such immensity,
that Voyager will bring a tear
of interspecies empathy

at the compulsion which sent forth
an envoy from a vanished race,
its science, politics, and art
long vaporized without a trace

except for this. For now, sail on,
space wanderer, fulfill your fate
as relic of a vanished planet,
singular, self-ultimate.

Shotgun Wedding

I

Three persons stand before a judge. The bride,
a farmer's daughter, virtue past repair,
now beams up at the man she stands beside,
a piece of hay still clinging to her hair.
The groom, a traveling salesman, finds his knees
atremble as he wonders at the lack
of luck that has him stammering I-take-thee's
encouraged by a shotgun in his back.

The father of the bride nods as the judge
proclaims them man and wife. The movie ends,
not saying if the new-made spouse will trudge
behind a plow the balance of his days
or flee, resume his city-slicker ways,
and share the tale someday with drunken friends.

II

What shotguns aimed at us compelled our vows
to lives demanded of us? What force curbed
contrary predilections? As the laws
enacted by our parents were absorbed,
what kept them in us—fear of punishment,
a father disappointed in his son,
a daughter shamed if she would not relent—
until ours were the hands that held the gun?

No matter, something harnessed us to places,
jobs, or people, ordering our lives.
Some soon accepted; some kicked at the traces
like peevish mules. With luck, something survives
the dull resentment at the barrel's shove,
and then one day we find we are in love.

To a Dying Artist

My father, retired from medicine, and living
in a nursing home,
was asked by a nervous friend there, "Tell me, Leon,
am I dying?"
"Yes, Mary," he told her, "We all are."

And true, we die, all of us, sooner or later,
but in your case,
with your cancer resurfacing, it looks like sooner.
The test results,
you wrote me last week, don't look promising.

Hearing this, I replied with words of cheer—
hang in there;
where there's life, there's hope, etcetera.
But let's assume
you're right about a soon-occurring death.

You and I long ago left the religion
in which we were raised.
Neither of us can now persuade himself
some eternal being
will show up at the moment of our deaths

and loft us to heaven, though if you undergo
a deathbed conversion,
I won't think the less of you; take consolation
where you find it,
the old faith or a new one if it gives meaning.

Given our pick, we might choose a sudden death
        like Vito Corleone's
in *The Godfather,* felled by a heart attack
in his garden,
doing labor he loved. A quick stab of pain,

then falling forward to the welcoming ground
and into darkness,
perhaps a final thought—*Goodbye, Carmella*—
and the last sensations
the smell of earth and a bird singing overhead.

But a man with time to see his death approaching,
like Robert Jordan
in the final scene of *For Whom the Bell Tolls,*
lying in ambush,
determined to take at least one of the fascists with him,

strikes a chord in the hearts of men like us.
To face an enemy
destined to win, and yet to not give up,
to go *mano a mano,*
the triumph in the struggle, not the outcome,

seems a noble thing. Alas, we know too well
that a little-noticed,
unheroic, drug-assisted slide
        into nothing
is the destiny that probably awaits us.

Many who care about you will pay visits
before then.
Accept well-meaning words with graciousness,
and be patient:
let that be your parting gift to them.

But you will also need to be alone,
      to sift with care
the life you're leaving. Here's hoping you achieve
the hardest peace,
the one that comes when you forgive yourself.

"A dying man needs to die," wrote Stewart Alsop
"as a sleepy man needs
to sleep, and there comes a time when it is wrong
as well as useless
to resist." Oh, Vernon, *mi amigo,*

your offspring, flesh-and-blood and paint-on-canvas,
will mark your place.
If you're awake when the final moment comes,
gather yourself.
Then exhale, and let your spirit fly.

Lights Out

The float engages as the toilet's tank
is filled. The sound of running water dies.
All noise of human bustle gone, the house
relaxes into weary creaks and sighs.

The trees outside are silent, with no wind
stirring their leaves. A sparrow in its nest,
I settle into sleep beneath the distant
rumble of a red-eye heading west.

The smoke detector's indicator light
winks faintly overhead, its tiny sun
the only glow except the bedside clock
displaying unwatched minutes one by one.

My breathing scarcely stirs the coverlet.
With no external sound distracting me,
I listen to my nervous system play
its steady note—F above middle C.

O let my end be gentle as this night
as silent and enfolding. No more dawn—
let darkness rock me in its arms until
my heartbeat slows, then stutters, then is gone.

About the Author

Reagan Upshaw was born raised in Texas. He attended Texas Tech University and the University of Chicago. He has made his living as an art dealer and art appraiser in New York. His articles, essays, and reviews of art and literature have appeared in *Art in America, The Magazine Antiques, Poets & Writers, The San Francisco Chronicle, The Washington Post,* and numerous other publications.

www.ingramcontent.com/pod-product-compliance
Lightning Source LLC
Chambersburg PA
CBHW072200160426
43197CB00012B/2469